For Him all Stars

15 CAROLS FOR UPPER VOICES

T0057493

MUSIC DEPARTMENT

OXFORD
UNIVERSITY PRESS

OXFORD
UNIVERSITY PRESS

Great Clarendon Street, Oxford OX2 6DP, England
198 Madison Avenue, New York, NY,10016, USA

Oxford University Press is a department of the University of Oxford.
It furthers the University's aim of excellence in research, scholarship,
and education by publishing worldwide

Oxford is a registered trade mark of Oxford University Press
in the UK and in certain other countries

© Oxford University Press 2006

The moral rights of the composers have been asserted

Database right Oxford University Press (maker)

First published 2006

All rights reserved. No part of this publication may be reproduced,
stored in a retrieval system, or transmitted, in any form or by any means,
without the prior permission in writing of Oxford University Press,
or as expressly permitted by law. Enquiries concerning reproduction
outside the scope of the above should be sent to the Music Copyright
Department, Oxford University Press, at the address above

Permission to perform the works in this anthology in public
(except in the course of divine worship) should normally be obtained
from the Performing Right Society Ltd. (PRS), 29/33 Berners Street,
London W1T 3AB, or its affiliated Societies in each country throughout
the world, unless the owner or the occupier of the premises
being used holds a licence from the Society

Permission to make a recording must be obtained in advance
from the Mechanical-Copyright Protection Society Ltd. (MCPS),
Elgar House, 41 Streatham High Road, London SW16 1ER,
or its affiliated Societies in each country throughout the world

3 5 7 9 10 8 6 4 2

ISBN 978-0-19-335569-9

Music and text origination by
Barnes Music Engraving Ltd., East Sussex
Printed in Great Britain on acid-free paper by
Halstan & Co. Ltd., Amersham, Bucks.

Contents

1. Balulalow — 4
   Antony Baldwin

2. Ring the bells — 7
   Alan Bullard

3. Scots Nativity — 15
   Alan Bullard

4. For him all stars have shone — 21
   Bob Chilcott

5. We Three Camels — 29
   David Hamilton

6. Cradle Song — 35
   Cecilia McDowall

7. Vulcan — 40
   Jenny McLeod

8. Tomorrow shall be my dancing day — 46
   Trad., arr. Malcolm Pearce

9. Mary's Cradle Song — 53
   Max Reger, arr. Paul Keene

10. Love came down at Christmas — 59
    John Rutter

11. Into this world, this day did come — 63
    Howard Skempton

12. There is no rose — 66
    Alan Smith

13. Carol of Our Lady — 70
    Christopher Wiggins

14. Remember, O thou man — 75
    Jonathan Willcocks

15. A Catch by the Hearth — 84
    Roderick Williams

in memoriam Susan Baldwin, 25 December 1986

1. Balulalow

Wedderburn, *Ane Compendious Bulk of Godly and Spiritual Sangis* (Edinburgh, 1567)

ANTONY BALDWIN
(b. 1957)

* If using piano, the low F and C in bars 20 and 21 should be played up an octave (see cue notes).

Original version for SATB and organ © Royal School of Church Music, 1992. This version © 2001 and 2006, Oxford University Press, Inc. Reproduced by permission. Photocopying this copyright material is ILLEGAL.

11
heart, and ne - ver, ne - ver mair from thee de - part.
14
div. mf
2. But I shall praise thee e - ver -
Sw. 8', 4'
mp
with sang - is sweet
17
- more with sang - is sweet un - to thy

20
ardente
f
gloir, the knees of my heart shall I
f
22
poco meno mosso
p
unis.
ten.
bow, and sing that richt ba - lu - la -
Sw.
(str., fl.) p
ten.
24
a tempo
rall.
- low.
opt. solo 8' (different tone from bar 1)
pp
soft 32'

7 March 1999

2. Ring the bells

Frances Jane Crosby (1820–1915)

ALAN BULLARD
(b. 1947)

© Oxford University Press 2006. Photocopying this copyright material is ILLEGAL.

10
with a song.
Wake your harps, ye
f
f
13
div. a 2
an - gels bright;
Sing a-loud ye hosts of light:
mp
16
mf cresc.
1.
Sing as on that ho - ly night:
Glo - ry in the
f
mf cresc.
2.
Sing, sing as on that ho - ly night:
Glo - ry
f
cresc.
f

19
high - - - est!
in the high - est!
f
p
22
p floating
Ring the bells of
mp espress.
Ring the bells of Christ - mas Day,
pp espress.
poco
25
Christ - mas Day, Through the air,
Waft the sto - ry far a - way; Through the air, the
poco

28
and the sea, Christ has come our
earth, the sea, Christ has come our
30
mf
life to be.
f
Wake your harps, ye an - gels
mf
life to be.
f
Wake your harps, ye
cresc.
f
Ped.
33
bright; Sing a - loud ye hosts of light:
an - gels bright; Sing a-loud ye hosts of light:

36
mf cresc.
f
Sing as on that ho - ly night: Glo - ry in the
mf cresc.
f
Sing, sing as on that ho - ly night: Glo - ry
mf cresc.
39
p
high - - - est! Ring the bells of
p
in the high - est! Ring the bells of
p
42
mf
love and peace, Ring the bells till time shall cease;
mf
love and peace, Ring the bells till time shall cease;
mf

45
mp
cresc.
Lo, he comes with us to dwell: Christ the Lord Im-
mp
cresc.
Lo, he comes with us to dwell: Christ the Lord Im-
mp
48
- man - u - el.
div. a 3
- man - u - el.
cresc.
f
Ped.
51
ff
1.
Wake your harps, ye an - gels bright; Sing a-loud ye
ff
2.
Wake your harps, ye an - gels bright; Sing a-
ff
3.
Wake your harps, ye an - gels bright;
ff

54
ff
hosts of light: Sing as on that
- loud ye hosts of light: Sing, sing as
Sing a - loud ye hosts of light: Sing, sing,
57
ho - ly night: Glo - ry in the high - - -
on that ho - ly night: Glo - ry in the high -
sing as on that ho - ly night: Glo - ry in the
dim.
Ped.

60
senza rall.
mf
ff
f
ff
- est! Ring the bells, ring the bells, ring the
mf
ff
f
ff
- est! Ring the bells, ring the bells, ring the
mf
ff
f
ff
high - est! Ring the bells, ring the bells, ring the
senza rall.
8va
p
ff sub.
63
fff
bells!
fff
bells!
fff
bells!
fff
Ped.

for Jan and Mary

3. Scots Nativity

Scottish trad.

ALAN BULLARD
(b. 1947)

This piece (T134) is available separately, and also in a version for SATB and piano (X446).

© Oxford University Press 2002 and 2006. Photocopying this copyright material is ILLEGAL.

15
lov - ing and kind, Shall now re - joice both
bairn so lov - ing Shall now re - joice both
19
poco tenuto
a tempo
p
heart and mind; Ba - low, lam-my, ba -
heart and mind; Ba - low, lam-my, ba -
poco tenuto
a tempo
p
23
p
-loo - ba - low.
ah
mp
-loo - ba - low.
And now shall

27
poco
ah
poco
Ma - ry's lit - tle boy For - ev - er
poco
31
f
E - ter - nal
be our hope and joy; E - ter - nal
f
f
35
be his reign here on earth, Re -
be his reign, his reign here on

38
poco tenuto
p
- joice then all peo - ple, for this ho - ly birth; Ba -
earth, Re - joice for this ho - ly birth; Ba -
poco tenuto
p
42
a tempo
- low, lam-my, ba - loo - ba - low.
- low, lam-my, ba - loo - ba - low.
a tempo
46
rit.
a tempo
p
Sleep gent - ly, sweet Je - sus, and
Sleep gent - ly, sweet Je - sus, and
rit.
a tempo
p

50
cresc.
know no fear, Thy sub - jects a - dor - ing watch
cresc.
know no fear, Thy sub - jects a - dor - ing watch
cresc.
54
f
o - ver thee here; God's an - gels and shep - herds and
f
o - ver thee here; God's an - - gels and
f
58
kine in their stall, And wise men and Vir - gin, Thy
shep - - herds, And wise men and Vir - gin, Thy

August 2001

bairn child; *kine* cattle; *Balow, lammy, baloobalow* Sleep, my little lamb

4. For him all stars have shone

Elizabeth Jennings

BOB CHILCOTT
(b. 1955)

The original version of this piece for upper-voice choir, SATB, and piano is available separately (BC57).

Text taken from 'The Shepherds' by Elizabeth Jennings; by permission of David Higham Associates. Music © Oxford University Press 2002 and 2006. Photocopying this copyright material is ILLEGAL.

8
stars bow down
The fierce winds ease their breath,
11
And care-ful shep - herds look u-pon the one un-sul - lied
TUTTI SOPRANOS and ALTOS
14
mp espress.
div.
birth.
They kneel and_ stare___ while time seems gone___ And
mp espress.

17
unis.
rit.
a tempo
good-ness rules the earth.
mp più espress.
21
S.1
S.2
SOPRANO 1 & 2
pp
He is so small the
A.1
A.2
ALTO 1 & 2
pp
poco cresc.
pp
24
stars bow down
The fierce winds ease their breath,

27
cresc.
And care-ful shep-herds look u-pon the one un-sul - lied
cresc.
cresc.
30
mp espress.
S.1
birth. They kneel and_ stare while time_ seems
mp espress.
S.2
birth. They kneel and_ stare while time seems gone And
mp espress.
A.1
A.2
birth. They kneel and_ stare while time seems gone And
mp espress.

33
rit.
a tempo
gone, gone, gone.
good-ness rules the earth.
unis.
good-ness rules the earth.
rit.
a tempo
p dolce e sost.
37
unis. p dolce
S.1
S.2
The blight on man is all un-done, And there will be no

40
mp cresc.
S.1
S.2
death, For though this child will be nailed on a cross, he'll
A.1
A.2
For though this child will be nailed on a cross, he'll
43
f
mf dim.
be so since he is the jewel of un - told worth,
be so since he is the jewel of un - told
be so since he is the jewel of
be so since he is the

46
rit.
a tempo
p legato espress.
For him all
worth,
un - told worth,
p legato espress.
For him all
pp
p legato espress.
jewel of un - told worth,
For him all stars have
rit.
a tempo
p
50
stars have shone,
For him all stars have shone,
pp
For him all
p legato espress.
all stars have shone,
all stars have shone,
stars have shone,
stars have shone,
shone,
pp
For him all
pp
shone,
stars have shone,
For him all stars have
pp

54
rit.
a little slower
p
stars have shone, for him all stars have shone, have
pp
all stars have shone, shone, have shone,
div.
p
stars have shone, stars have shone, have shone,
p
shone, stars have shone, have shone,
rit.
a little slower
58
rit.
shone, shone.
unis.
shone, shone.
shone, shone.
shone, shone.
rit.
p dolce
pp

5. We Three Camels

Jane Yolen

DAVID HAMILTON
(b. 1955)

We Three Camels by Jane Yolen; used by permission of Curtis Brown, Ltd. Copyright © 1991. All rights reserved. Music © Oxford University Press 2006. Photocopying this copyright material is ILLEGAL.

8
f
king look back. 'For-ward!' he cried, 'We fol-low the star, we
f
king look back. 'For-ward!' he cried, 'We fol-low the star, we
f
king look back. 'For-ward!' he cried, 'For-ward we fol-low the star, we
f
11
p
do not stop.' So here we are.
p
do not stop.' So here we are.
p
do not stop.' So here we are.
p

14
p
oo
mp
I car-ried a king, but not the One, through
mp
I car-ried a king, but not the One,
mp
17
oo
oo
sear-ing heat and blind-ing sun, through nights so cold my
through sear-ing heat and blind-ing sun, through nights so cold,

20
f
and slaves wrapped cloths a - bout my toes. But
f
nos - trils froze, and slaves wrapped cloths a - bout my toes. But
f
nos - trils froze, and slaves wrapped cloths a - bout my toes. But
f

23
for - ward we went led by a star. We did not stop,
for - ward we went led by a star. We did not stop,
for - ward we went, but for - ward led by a star. We did not stop,

26
mp
mf
so here we are. I car-ried a king, but
mp
mf
so here we are. I car-ried a king, but
mp
mf
so here we are. but
mp
mf
30
not the Babe, and al - so box - es jewel in-laid. My packs were stuffed with
not the Babe, and al - so box - es jewel in-laid. My packs were stuffed with
not the Babe, and al - so box - es jewel in-laid. My packs were stuffed with

34
f
scents and spice, the grand-est la - dies to en-tice. No la-dies saw we, but
f
scents and spice, the grand-est la - dies to en-tice No la-dies saw we, but
f
scents and spice, the grand-est la - dies to en-tice. No_ la-dies saw we, no la-dies,
f
38
rit.
p
on-ly a star. We did not stop, so here we_____ are.
p
on-ly a star. We did not stop, so here we are.
p
on-ly a star. We did not stop, so here we are.
rit.
p

6. Cradle Song

William Blake

CECILIA McDOWALL
(b. 1951)

© Oxford University Press 2006. Photocopying this copyright material is ILLEGAL.

11
joys of night: Sleep, sleep,
joys of night: Sleep, sleep,
p
p
p warm
16
in thy sleep Lit - tle sor - rows
in thy sleep Lit - tle sor - rows
p
p
cresc.
dim.
p
20
sit and weep.
sit and weep.
Ped.

24
mp
Sweet Babe, in thy face
mp
Sweet Babe, in thy face
p
con Ped.
Ped.
29
mf
Soft de - sires I can trace,
mf
Soft de - sires I can trace,
mf
con Ped.
34
mp
Se - cret joys and se - cret smiles,
mp
Se - cret joys and se - cret
p

38
mp
Lit - tle pret - ty in - fant wiles.
mp
smiles, Lit - tle pret - ty in - fant wiles.
mp
cresc.
43
mf
Cun - ning wiles that creep
mf
O the cun - ning wiles that creep
mf
Ped.
con Ped.
48
In thy lit - tle heart a - sleep:
In thy lit - tle heart a - sleep:

53
mp
When thy lit - tle heart does wake,
mp
When thy lit - tle heart does wake,
mp
57
cresc.
Then the dread - ful night
cresc.
Then the dread - ful night
cresc.
61
mf
p dolce
rit.
pp
shall break.
mf
p dolce
pp
shall break.
rit.
8va
mf
pp dolce
dim.
ppp
una corda
Ped.

7. Vulcan

Words and music by
JENNY McLEOD
(b. 1941)

© Oxford University Press 2006. Photocopying this copyright material is ILLEGAL.

13
S.1
near, look you.
shi - ning light.
migh - ti - est.
A king is ri - sen from
S.2
f
This is the high mid-night Of all the year.
Where-of his ma - jes - ty Has no dec - li - ning.
In him the migh - ti - est Of migh-ty pow - ers.
A king is
A.
mf
(1.–3.) A king is ri - sen from
ff
18
f
the quar - ter of the sun. Now Rex Pa - ci - fi - cus
ri - sen from the quar-ter of the sun. Now Rex Pa - ci - fi - cus
f
the quar - ter of the sun. Now Rex Pa - ci - fi - cus

Exultet coelum laudibus Let Heaven rejoice with praises; *Agnoscat omne saeculum* Let every age and nation know

33
Out from the o - rient crys - tal sky is y come!
Ex - ul - tet coe - lum lau - di - bus, is y come!
Ag - nos - cat om - ne sae - cu - lum is y come!
o - - rient crys - tal sky is y come!
coe - - lum lau - di - bus, is y come!
om - - ne sae - cu - lum is y come!
o - - rient crys - tal sky is y come!
coe - - lum lau - di - bus, is y come!
om - - ne sae - cu - lum is y come!
f
39
x 3
mf
Peo-ple, look east, look you.
mf
Peo-ple, look east, look you.
x 3
mf
mp

gloria tibi glory to you

57
1.
-a ti - bi, is y come!
glo-ri-a ti - bi, is y come!
glo-ri-a ti - bi, is y come!
1.
f
61b
2.
come!
come!
come!
2.
f
68
mf
mp
RH
Ped.

to Elizabeth

8. Tomorrow shall be my dancing day

English trad.
arr. MALCOLM PEARCE
(b. 1950)

A version of Malcolm Pearce's arrangement for SATB and organ is available separately (X461).

© Oxford University Press 2005 and 2006. Photocopying this copyright material is ILLEGAL.

12
call my true love to my dance. Sing
mf
15
O my love, O my love, my love, my love, This
f
18
have I done for my true love.
dim.
22
SOPRANOS only
mp
S.
Then was I born of a vir - gin pure; Of
legato
pp
Man.

25
her I took flesh - ly sub-stance. Thus was I knit to
28
man's na - ture, To call my true love to my dance.
cresc.
Ped.
31
S.
mf
Sing O my love, O my love, my
A.
mf
Sing O my love, O my love, my
mf

34
love, my love, This have I done for my true love.
love, my love, sing O for my true love.
37
mp dolce
mf
ah
In a man - ger laid and
p sempre legato
dim.
Ch. (Gt.) solo
41
ah
wrapp'd I was, So ve - ry poor this was my chance, Be -

44
(ah) ah
-twixt an ox and a sil - ly poor ass, To call my true love to my dance.
cresc.
(Sw.)
48
f
Sing O my love, O my love, my love, my love, This
f
Sing O my love, O my love, my love, my love, This
f
52
have I done for my true love.
have I done for my true love.
Gt.

55
58
S.
A.
unis.
f
To - mor-row shall be my dan - cing day; I
tr
7
Gt.
62
would my true love did so chance To see the le - gend
65
of my play, To call my true love to my dance.

68
div.
(tr)
Sing O my love, O my love, my
71
unis.
love, my love, This have I done for my true love,
dim.
Sw.
74
mf
mp
for my true love,
for my true love,
78
p
unis.
for my true love.
Ch.(Gt.)
tr
p

9. Mary's Cradle Song

MAX REGER (1873–1916)
arr., with English text, by Paul Keene

This piece is available separately (W116).

* The alto part is optional, though desirable. If it is omitted, soprano 2 should sing the lowest part in bars 64–6.

© Oxford University Press 1995 and 2006. Photocopying this copyright material is ILLEGAL.

13
sweet - ly now sings a bird up - on the bough:
16
p
'Sleep, ba - by, sleep, dear one,
pp
20
sleep, Je - sus, sleep.'
espress.
p
24
mp
S.1
2. Joy - ful is thy laugh - ter now, peace - ful is thy si - lent rest.
mp
S.2/A.
2. Joy - ful is thy laugh - ter now, and peace - ful is thy rest.

28
cresc.
mf
Yet, a-cross thy tran - quil brow soon will ro - ses' thorns be press'd.
cresc.
mf
Yet, a-cross thy tran - quil brow soon will ro - ses' thorns be press'd.
espress.
cresc.
mf
32
p
Sleep, ba - by, sleep,
p
Sleep now, sleep
p
dolce
36
dear one, sleep, Je - sus, sleep.
now, sleep, Je - sus, sleep.
espress.
Ped.

41
S.1
p
3. As
S.2
pp sempre, sognante
mm
mm
A.
pp sempre, sognante
mm
ppp dolciss.
(Ped.)
46
eve - ning falls the sun - light goes, the ro - ses now their pe - tals close.
mm
mm
(Ped.)

50
Je - sus, lay thy head in rest sweet - ly on thy mo - ther's breast,
(mm)
mm
mm
mm
poco cresc.
dim.
Ped.
54
p
and through thy dreams will waft Ma - ry's cra - dle song so soft:
(pp)
mm
(pp)
mm
pp
Ped.

59
pp
'Ah,
'Ah,
(mm) 'Ah,
ah,
espress.
dolciss.
64
pochiss. ritenuto
a tempo
rit.
sleep, Je - sus, sleep.'
sleep, Je - sus, sleep.'
sleep, Je - sus, sleep.'
pochiss. ritenuto
a tempo
rit.
ppp

10. Love came down at Christmas

Christina Rossetti (1830–94)

JOHN RUTTER
(b. 1945)

This carol is also available in its original version, for mixed voices (X224). The orchestral accompaniment, for strings, may be used with either version, and is available on hire.

© Oxford University Press 1971 and 2006. Photocopying this copyright material is ILLEGAL.

14
SOLO VOICE
or SEMI-CHORUS
A
mp legato
2. Wor - ship we the God - head, Love in - car - nate,
S.1
S.2
p
mm
mm
A.1/A.2
p
mm
mm
A
(Ped.)
18
cresc.
mf
Love di-vine; Wor - ship we our Je - sus: But where-with for
cresc.
mp
mm
aw
cresc.
mp
mm
aw
cresc.
mp
(Man.)

22
mp
sa - cred sign? But where-with for sa - cred sign?
p
mm
p
mm
p
(Ped.)
(Man.)
B
26
p
S.1
S.2
3. Love shall be our to - ken, Love be yours and
A.1
A.2
p
Love be yours and
B
(Man.)

30
cresc.
love be mine; Love to God and all men,
cresc.
33
mf
p
Love for plea and gift and sign; Love for plea and
mf
p
36
poco rall.
gift and sign.
gift and sign.
poco rall.
pp
(Ped.)

11. Into this world, this day did come

English trad.

HOWARD SKEMPTON
(b. 1947)

© Oxford University Press 2006. Photocopying this copyright material is ILLEGAL.

39
make us that were poor in - deed, Rich with - out a - ny need,
47
mf
tru - ly. I pray you, be mer - ry and sing_ with me In wor -
mf
56
(mf)
- ship of Christ's Na - ti - vi - ty. 3. A sta - ble was his cham - ber; a cratch was his
(mf)
63
bed; He had not a pil - low to lay un - der his head. With mai - den's milk that
70
mp
mf
babe was fed, In poor clothes was lapped the Lord Al - might - y. I
mp
mf

cratch crib

78
pray you, be mer - ry and sing_ with me In wor - ship of Christ's Na -
87
(mf)
-ti - vi - ty. 4. A no - ble les - son here is us taught, To set all world
(mf)
96
ri - ches at naught, But pray we that we may be thi - ther
103
brought, where ri - ches is e - ver - last - ing - ly. I pray you, be mer -
113
rit.
-ry and sing_ with me In wor - ship of Christ's Na - ti - vi - ty.

12. There is no rose

15th-cent.

ALAN SMITH
(b. 1962)

Res miranda A wonderful thing

Original version for SATB unaccompanied. © 2006 Oxford University Press, Inc. Reproduced by permission. Photocopying this copyright material is ILLEGAL.

Paresforma Of the same form

Gloria in excelsis Deo Glory to God on high; *Gaudeamus* Let us rejoice

35
mp
birth: Tran - se - a - - - - mus.
mp
(mm) Tran - se - a - mus, Tran - se -
mp
(mm) Tran - se - a - mus,
p
39
sempre rall.
p
pp morendo div.
- a - mus, Tran - se - a - mus.
p
pp morendo
Tran - se - a - mus, Tran - se - a - mus.
sempre rall.
pp morendo

13. Carol of Our Lady

Medieval

CHRISTOPHER WIGGINS
(b. 1956)
op. 143 no. 3

© Oxford University Press 2006. Photocopying this copyright material is ILLEGAL.

11
peer, Ma - ry, flow'r of wo - men all,
sing: For she with her mai - den - hood,
peer, Ma - ry, flow'r of wo - men all,
sing: For she with her mai - den - hood,
peer, Ma - ry, flow'r of wo - men all,
sing: For she with her mai - den - hood,
17
1.
Chri - stè's mo - ther dear.
Have our heav'n - ly King.
Chri - stè's mo - ther dear.
Have our heav'n - ly King.
Chri - stè's mo - ther dear.
Have our heav'n - ly King.
1.

22b
2.
più f
poco
Brought now forth our Sa - viour in the win - ter-ing,
più f
poco
Brought now forth our Sa - viour in the win - ter-ing,
più f
poco
Brought now forth our Sa - viour in the win - ter-ing,
2.
più f
mf
28
mf
Where-fore now with great joy - ing To this
mf
Where-fore now with great joy - ing To this
mf
Where-fore now with great joy - ing To this

34
f
La - dy we now sing. Where-fore now with
f
La - dy we now sing. Where-fore now with
f
La - dy we now sing. Where-fore now with
f
39
great joy - ing and with wit - tes clear
great joy - ing and with wit - tes clear
great joy - ing and with wit - tes clear

44
ff
Do we this La - dy
ff
Do we this La - dy
ff
Do we this La - dy
ff
49
mp
p
prais - ing in our best man - ner.
mp
p
prais - ing in our best man - ner.
mp
p
prais - ing in our best man - ner.
mp
pp

14. Remember, O thou man

Thomas Ravenscroft? (*c.*1582–1635)

JONATHAN WILLCOCKS
(b. 1953)

© Oxford University Press 2006. Photocopying this copyright material is ILLEGAL.

17
mp
thou art dead and gone, and I did what I can: there-fore re - pent.
mp
p
23
S.1
mf
Sing, an - gels sing.
S.2
f
2. The an - gels all did sing, O thou man, O thou man, The
A.
mf
Sing, an - gels sing.
f
29
Sing, an - gels sing. Sing, an - gels sing, sing
an - gels all did sing up - on the hill; The an - gels all did sing, sing
Sing, an - gels sing. Sing, an - gels sing, sing
f

35
unis.
f
dim.
p
S.
praise to our hea-ven-ly King, and peace to all liv-ing with a good will.
A.
praise to our hea-ven-ly King, and peace to all liv-ing with a good will.
40
mp
3. To Beth-lem did they go, O thou
.1
ah
.2
ah

45
man, O thou man, To Beth-lem did they go the shep - herds
(ah) ah
(ah) ah
p
50
mf
three, To Beth-lem did they go to see whereit was so, if
mf
ah ah
mf
ah
mf

55
p
Christ were born or no, to set us free.
p
(ah)
p
ah
p
60
A.
unis. mf
4. In Beth - lem he was born, O thou man, O thou man, In
mf
65
Beth - lem he was born for all our sakes, In

69
div.
S.
A.
f
Beth - lem he was born for us that were for - lorn, and
73
unis.
p
there-fore took no scorn, our flesh to take.
78
mf warmly
5. Give thanks to God al - way, O thou

83
div. S.
A.
man, O thou man, Give thanks to God al - way most joy - ful -
88
f
- ly, Give thanks to God al - way for this our hap - py
f
92
mf cresc.
day, let us all
mf cresc.
day, let us all sing,
mf cresc.
day, let us all sing,
mf cresc.
day, let us all sing,
mf cresc.

96
f
sing, let us all sing and say: 'Ho - ly, ho -
let us all sing and say: 'Ho - ly, ho -
let us all sing and say: 'Ho - ly, ho -
let us all sing and say: 'Ho - ly, ho -
mf
102
p
- ly, ho - ly!'
- ly, ho - ly!'
- ly, ho - ly!'
- ly, ho - ly!'

108
unis. p
A.
6. Re - mem - ber, O thou man, O thou man, O thou man, Re -
113
-mem - ber, O thou man, thy time is spent: Re - mem - ber, O thou man, how
119
pp
thou art dead and gone, and I did what I can: there-fore re - pent.
pp
124
rall.

for Richard Vendome and the Oxford Girls' Choir

15. A Catch by the Hearth

English trad.

RODERICK WILLIAMS
(b. 1965)

* During the piece, the choir divides into 2, 3, and eventually 4 parts. Each time the choir should be split evenly.

© Oxford University Press 2006. Photocopying this copyright material is ILLEGAL.

30
1.
Sing we all mer - ri - ly Christ-mas is here,
2.
Sing we all mer - ri - ly Christ - mas is here, The day that
3.
Bring forth the hol-ly, The box, and the bay, Deck_ out our cot-tage For glad_
35
The day that we love_ best of the days___ in the year.___
we love_ best of the days in the year._____
Christ-mas Day, Christ-mas Day, for Christ - mas Day.
42
unis.
Sing we all mer - ri - ly___ Draw a - round___ the fire,_____
46
div. a 4
Sis - ter and bro - ther,_____ Grand - sire, and sire.

50
1.
Sing we all mer - ri - ly Draw a - round the fire,
2.
Sing we all mer - ri - ly Christ-mas is here,
3.
Sing we all mer - ri - ly Christ - mas is here, The day that
4.
Bring forth the hol-ly, The box, and the bay, Deck out our cot-tage For glad
55
Sis - ter and bro - - ther, Grand - sire, and sire,
The day that we love best of the days in the year,
we love best of the days in the year, of the
Christ-mas Day, Christ-mas Day, for Christ - mas
60
poco decresc.
f
grand - sire, and sire. Sing we mer - ri - ly Christ - mas is here.
poco decresc.
f
of the days in the... Sing we mer - ri - ly Christ - mas is here.
poco decresc.
f
days in the year. Sing we mer - ri - ly Christ-mas is here.
poco decresc.
f
Day, Christ - mas... Sing we mer - ri - ly Christ - mas is here.